D

BG

WORM'S EYE VIEW

BY KIPCHAK JOHNSON
ILLUSTRATIONS BY THOMPSON YARDLEY

WORM'S EYE VIEW

THE MILLBROOK PRESS · BROOKFIELD, CONNECTICUT

Cataloging-in-Publication Data

Johnson, Kipchak.
Worm's eye view: make your own wildlife refuge/by
Kipchak Johnson; illustrations by Thompson Yardley.
Brookfield, Conn.: The Millbrook Press, 1991.
40 p.: col. ill; cm (A lighter look book)
Includes bibliographical references
Summary: Discusses ways to attract wildlife in the backyard and the role of wild plants and animals in ecology.
1. Wildlife—Juvenile literature.   2. Predation
(Biology)—Juvenile literature.   3. Insect-plant
relationships—Juvenile literature.   4. Pesticides and
wildlife—Juvenile literature.   I. Yardley, Thompson,
ill.   II. Title.   III. Series.
574.5
ISBN 1-878841-30-0

First published in the United States in 1991 by
The Millbrook Press Inc.
2 Old New Milford Road
Brookfield, Connecticut 06804
© Copyright Cassell plc 1990
First published in Great Britain in 1990 by
Cassell Publishers Limited

WORM'S EYE VIEW

THIS IS A WORM'S EYE VIEW

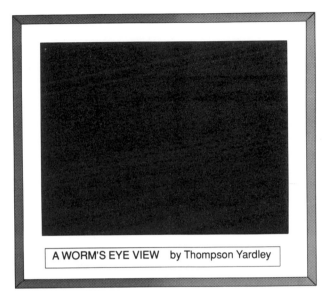

A WORM'S EYE VIEW   by Thompson Yardley

Worms don't have eyes, but they
can feel light through their skin.

USE YOUR EYES!

Find out how worms find their food!

Find out why plants need animals
and why animals need plants!

Find out how to make a wildlife refuge
and make friends with toads!

ANIMALS MUST GO!

One hundred years ago there were two billion people living on the Earth. Today there are five billion people! And people want a lot of space! They take land away from wild animals and plants to make houses, roads, factories, and farms.

WHAT YOU CAN DO

You can help wild animals by giving them a place to live.

Make a wildlife refuge in your back garden! Small animals will be happy to come and live there.

[8]

A WILDLIFE REFUGE!

To start your wildlife refuge, find a patch of ground that nobody uses. Perhaps there's a bit in a corner of your backyard.

Clear away any debris that's on it. Take a look at your soil. Is it sticky or crumbly, light or dark, moist or dry?

There are lots of different types of soil. The way soil looks and feels depends on what's in it.

WHAT SOIL IS MADE OF

HUMUS: This is the rotting remains of dead plants and animals. Humus provides food for plants that grow in the soil.

AIR: The gaps between bits of soil are full of air. Tiny creatures that live in the soil breathe this air.

WATER: This is needed by plants and animals.

SAND: Sand is just rock that has been broken down into fine grains over millions of years.

CLAY: Clay is rock that has become a fine powder. It feels like a smooth paste when mixed with water.

DEBRIS: You may also find bits of broken pottery, stones, bricks, bones, bottle tops, coins, and so on.

Cacti can live in dry sandy soil

Lythrum is a common plant that loves damp soil

Different types of plants like different types of soil. No matter what type of soil you have, some plants will come and grow there.

So will tiny creatures . . .

MEET THE MICROBES

The smallest living things are called microbes. They are too small to see without a powerful microscope. Many of them live in the soil.

CUP OF SOIL FACT
One cup of soil may contain more living creatures than there are people in the whole world!

ALGAE
Sometimes you can see green patches of algae on damp rocks and on the surface of the soil.

FUNGI
Mushrooms and toadstools are fungi. Many other types of fungi are too small to see. Fungi live on other plants and on animals.

Bacteria are very small. Imagine that just a single bacterium could grow to the size of the period at the end of this sentence. Then it would be 300 times its normal size. An average human being growing by this much would be about a third of a mile (half a kilometer) tall.

BACTERIA
These are tiny plants. When plants and animals die, they are eaten by bacteria. This is what is happening when dead things rot away.

PROTOZOA
These are the smallest animals. They eat some bacteria, and other types of bacteria eat them!

MITES AND WORMS

You may be able to see some tiny creatures without a microscope. Here are just a few of them . . .

SPIDER
Some spiders that live in the soil are very small. Some of them make webs, and some lie in wait for the animals they eat.

SPRINGTAIL
A type of insect that often lives under rocks. It leaps around when you lift its rock. Some springtails live in the soil. These have shorter legs, so they can't spring about. They eat fungi and humus.

MITES
There are hundreds of different mites in the soil. They have eight legs, and some of them look like tiny lobsters! They eat insects, plants, and nematode worms.

NEMATODE WORM
A worm that looks like a bit of thread. It eats bacteria and protozoa and other nematode worms!

WIREWORM
This isn't a real worm at all! It's the young of the click beetle. Gardeners hate it because it eats plant roots.

EARTHWORM
Perhaps the most important animal in the soil. It does an amazing amount of work. Take a look . . .

WORMS

Worms do more to make soil than any other creature.
It's all part of the exciting life of an earthworm!

Worms are male and female at the same time. But . . . two worms need to get together to mate.

After mating, each worm lays its eggs. Each worm then makes a slimy nest where the eggs hatch into new worms.

Worms don't lay eggs every day. Mostly they dig tunnels and eat a lot.

Some birds can pick worms out of the soil. Worms usually stay out of reach during the day.

WORM HAIR TEST
A worm has lots of tiny hairs on its skin. These help it to grip the soil. Gently pick up a worm. Put it in a glass bowl. It won't be able to climb the sides because its hairs can't grip the shiny glass.

Remember to put me back in the soil!

Worms often climb to the surface at night. They usually leave their tails in their wormholes, so that they can quickly escape from danger.

WORMS

The earthworm reaches out of its hole and pulls a leaf down from the surface.

The worm drags the leaf underground where it's safe to eat it. Some big worms go down as far as 10 feet (3 meters) from the surface.

Worms also eat soil as they make their tunnels. They digest the little bits of plant material in the soil and pass the rest out behind them.

Some worms leave their droppings on the surface. These droppings are often soil from deep down. They are called worm casts.

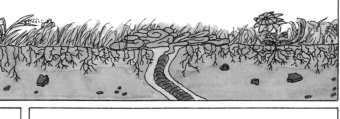

EARTHWORM EARTH FACT

20 tons of soil

All the worms in a grass field the size of a soccer field can move a truckload of soil in a year.

Worm tunnels help air and water reach the roots of plants. This also helps other soil creatures that need air and water.

That means worms turn the soil. They move deep soil to the surface and drag leaves underground. This helps to bring humus into the deep soil.

SPRING AND SEEDS

When spring comes, plants will grow in your wildlife refuge. Many plants grow from seeds. Some grow from pieces of root in the soil. Most seeds fall in the autumn and stay in the soil until spring.

Here are a few different types of seeds.

Poppy seeds

Dandelion seeds

Blackberry seeds

Grass seeds

Oak seed (acorn)

Maple seed

Burdock seed

HOW SEEDS ARRIVE IN YOUR WILDLIFE REFUGE

Some birds hide seeds to eat later on.

They sometimes forget where they've buried them. Then a new tree or another plant can grow from the seed.

Some seeds are so small you can hardly see them. Seeds this small may be carried in the air.

Some larger seeds, such as maple and dandelion seeds, are also blown by the wind.

Birds can't digest the seeds from some berries. So bird droppings might contain, for example, blackberry seeds.

Some seeds have hooks, which stick to animals as they brush past the plants. Then the seeds fall off the animal's fur and drop onto the soil.

The burdock plant has seeds like this.

Seeds from nearby plants can fall into tiny cracks and holes in the soil.

Why not add some wildflower seeds of your own?

A mixture of plants will be good for your wildlife refuge.

[14]

PLANTING WILDFLOWERS

It's not easy to find seeds by yourself.

And . . . there wouldn't be any wildflowers left in the countryside if everybody picked them.

Some plants are protected by law.

So . . . it's best to buy packets of wildflower seeds from a garden center.

Try to get a lot of different sorts of seeds in case some of them won't grow in your soil.

HOW TO PLANT WILDFLOWER SEEDS

| Make a hole about ¾ inch (2 cm) deep. | Drop a seed in the hole. | Cover the hole with soil and press down gently. |

Many wildflowers and weeds are quite tough. But you may need to water them when they're still small. Water them if the soil gets very dry.

FARMS AND WILDLIFE

Your wildlife refuge will give animals and wild plants a small place to live. Nowadays there are fewer and fewer wildflowers in the countryside. This is partly because farmers have plowed up more and more land to grow food crops.

Many wildflowers and animals used to live in meadows and other wild areas that have now been turned into fields for crops.

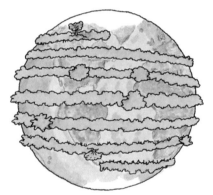

In Britain, for instance, many farm fields were once surrounded by thick hedges that provided homes for both wild animals and plants.

But since 1969, farmers have removed almost 140,000 miles (225,000 kilometers) of hedges, so that they can make their fields larger. That's enough to stretch six times around the world!

Rain and sunlight will help wildflowers grow in your wildlife refuge. But you'll have to be patient. Your plants won't grow as quickly as you'd like!

WEEDKILLERS

Some gardeners add strong poisons to the soil. These poisons then kill plants that the gardeners don't want.

But . . . some of these weedkillers are so strong that nothing will grow after the soil has been poisoned. The small animals that feed on the plants are also killed.

And . . . sometimes weedkillers used on plants are washed into the rivers and into our drinking water.
So make your wildlife refuge a weedkiller-free zone!

POISON FACT

Just a tiny dose of the weedkiller called paraquat can kill you.

Weedkillers can be dangerous for people as well as plants!

It's a good idea to grow lots of different kinds of plants in your wildlife refuge.

They will become food for many kinds of animals . . . especially insects.

INSECT INSPECTION

There are more than 700,000 different types of insects.
That's more than all the other types of animals put together! You can
be sure that lots of insects will come and live in your wildlife refuge.
Inspect your soil and plants. Here are some of the insects you may see.

APHID

Aphids live by sucking sap from the stems and leaves of plants. Gardeners don't like aphids because they weaken plants. Aphid droppings are a sort of sweet, sticky stuff that ants love. If you stand under an oak tree in summer, you'll get covered with tiny droplets of this fluid, which is called honeydew.

ANT

An ants' nest is a very well-organized home built in several layers, a bit like an apartment building. One nest can contain thousands of ants. The mound thrown up by ants when digging a nest is called an anthill.

BEE

Many bees live in nests in trees or in beekeepers' hives. They make honey from the nectar in flowers. Honeybees won't sting you unless you frighten them.

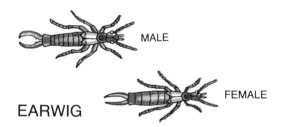

EARWIG

Earwigs look fierce, but they can't bite with their pincers. Earwigs like to rest in a hole during the day. But don't worry, they won't crawl into your ear hole!

COLORADO POTATO BEETLE

Bright colors often mean insects are poisonous to other creatures. The Colorado potato beetle eats potatoes, so its main enemies are farmers.

FIREFLY

Look for fireflies (sometimes called lightning bugs) after dark. They have a special chemical that allows them to send out flashes of light!

SOUTHERN TIGER MOTH
MONARCH BUTTERFLY

It's hard to tell the difference between moths and butterflies. Moths usually have fatter bodies, and many fly at night. Butterflies have little lumps on the end of their antennae and fly during the day.

WALKINGSTICK

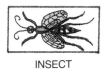

The walkingstick eats leaves. It keeps so still during the day that it looks like a dry twig. This saves it from being eaten by other animals.

LADYBIRD BEETLE

Ladybird beetles help gardeners by eating aphids, which can harm plants.

SPIDER FACT

SPIDER   INSECT

Spiders aren't insects. Insects have six legs, and spiders have eight. Most insects have wings. Spiders don't. Most spiders eat insects. But some insects, such as spider wasps, hunt for spiders!

THE POLLINATION PROCESS

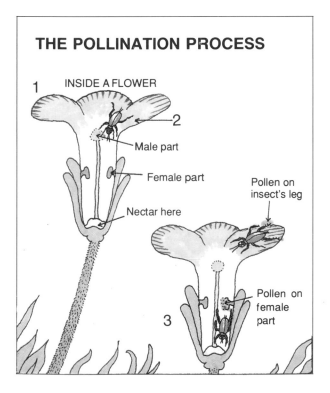

1 INSIDE A FLOWER

2

Male part

Female part

Nectar here

Pollen on insect's leg

Pollen on female part

3

Many plants need insects to help them produce seeds. Insects help through pollination. It works like this . . .

1. Most flowers contain male and female parts and a sweet liquid called nectar. Insects like nectar.

2. To get to the nectar, insects have to squeeze past the male part of the flower. The insect rubs a fine dust called pollen from the male part.

3. The insect then visits another flower. The male pollen falls from the insect onto the female part of the flower. This fertilizes the flower, so that a seed can be formed. Different flowers attract different creatures for pollination. The aspidistra plant is pollinated by snails!

SLUGS AND SNAILS

As your plants grow bigger, larger animals will come to feed on them.

Keep a look out for slugs and snails.

They belong to the same family of animals as octopuses!

Snails have rough tongues. If you're quiet, you can hear them eating!

People can eat some kinds of snails. But the sort you find in the garden aren't the ones you can eat!

Some birds like to eat garden snails. If you keep still, you might see a blackbird cracking one open!

Pick up a snail very gently. Place it in a glass bowl.

Watch the snail from underneath and see how it moves.

Be sure to put the snail back where you found it.

And don't forget to clean the bowl!

SLUGS AND SNAILS

A snail's shell helps to keep the snail from drying out.

Slugs are like snails without shells. They need to keep their skin damp, so they are covered in a sticky slime.

Slugs taste nasty, and so most birds won't eat them.

Gardeners don't like slugs and snails that eat garden plants.

To kill slugs, gardeners sometimes put poisonous slug pellets on the soil. When a slug eats one of these pellets, its body dries up and it dies.

SLUG DUNG FACT

Some slug experts say that slug droppings help the microbes that eat dead leaves.

Animals often eat our plants. But we shouldn't try to kill them with chemicals.

Slug pellets can kill other animals as well.

A bird that eats a poisoned snail will be poisoned too!

FLIES

Most small animals have lots of young. Some flies lay up to 3,000 eggs at a time! Imagine . . .

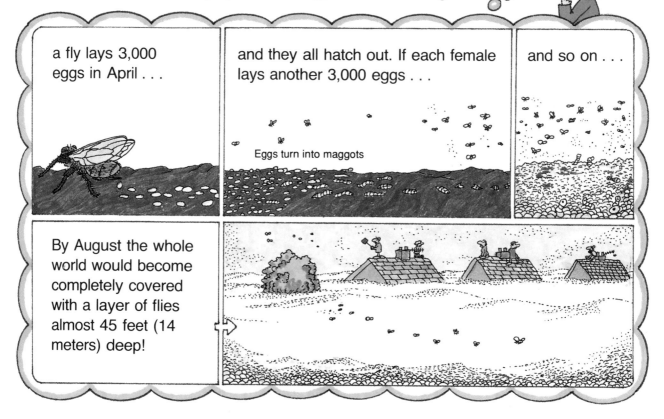

a fly lays 3,000 eggs in April . . .

and they all hatch out. If each female lays another 3,000 eggs . . .

Eggs turn into maggots

and so on . . .

By August the whole world would become completely covered with a layer of flies almost 45 feet (14 meters) deep!

But don't worry. This doesn't happen because . . .

1. There just isn't enough food for that many flies!

2. Other animals come along and eat the eggs and the flies.

Animals that eat other animals are called predators. Almost everything can be a meal for another creature . . .

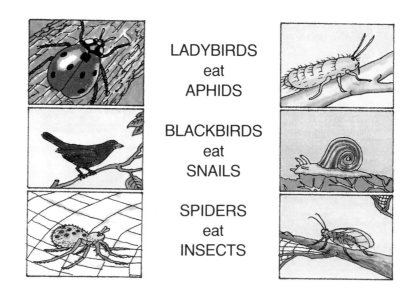

LADYBIRDS
eat
APHIDS

BLACKBIRDS
eat
SNAILS

SPIDERS
eat
INSECTS

PESTS

Some animals like to eat our food crops. Farmers grow huge fields full of wheat, potatoes, cabbages, and so on. This encourages large numbers of animals to move in and eat their favorite foods.

Some caterpillars like eating cabbages.

Predators move in to eat the caterpillars.

Gardeners and farmers call crop-eating animals pests.

When there's plenty of food to eat, the pests produce lots of young.

Then there are too many pests, and the predators can't eat them all.

Many farmers and gardeners spray their plants with pesticides. Pesticides are chemicals that kill pests. But . . . many pesticides kill the predators too!

APHID PEST FACT

A gardener once counted 24,688 aphids on a single tomato plant!

So . . . it's best not to use pesticides, especially in the garden. Your wildlife refuge can be a home for aphids and ladybirds too!

All sorts of other animals will come and live in your wildlife refuge if you grow enough different plants.

HABITATS

All living things need food, water, and a place to live. The area that an animal lives in is called its habitat. Each kind of animal likes to live in its own sort of habitat. Your wildlife refuge will provide lots of different habitats for small animals.

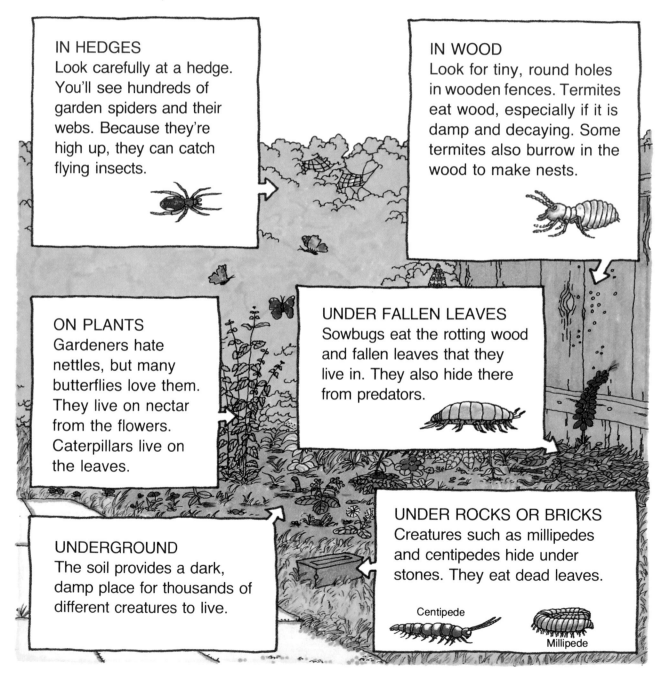

IN HEDGES
Look carefully at a hedge. You'll see hundreds of garden spiders and their webs. Because they're high up, they can catch flying insects.

IN WOOD
Look for tiny, round holes in wooden fences. Termites eat wood, especially if it is damp and decaying. Some termites also burrow in the wood to make nests.

ON PLANTS
Gardeners hate nettles, but many butterflies love them. They live on nectar from the flowers. Caterpillars live on the leaves.

UNDER FALLEN LEAVES
Sowbugs eat the rotting wood and fallen leaves that they live in. They also hide there from predators.

UNDERGROUND
The soil provides a dark, damp place for thousands of different creatures to live.

UNDER ROCKS OR BRICKS
Creatures such as millipedes and centipedes hide under stones. They eat dead leaves.

Centipede

Millipede

SUMMER HABITATS

Here's something you can do in summer when lots of animals are looking for a home.

Collect a few small piles of leaves, garden clippings, and other old items.

Put them on the edge of your wildlife refuge.

A PILE OF
LEAVES

A PILE OF
STICKS

SOME
BROKEN
BRICKS

AN OLD
BUCKET

A
BROKEN
TOY

AN OLD
SHIRT

Leave these homemade habitats for two weeks.

Then carefully take a look at the animals that have moved in.

Don't try wearing the shirt, though!

HOW ABOUT A GARDEN POND?

A garden pond will be a habitat for lots of animals.
It's best to start your wildlife pond in early summer.

Dig a hole in the ground.

Put an old dishpan in it.

Pack soil up to the rim of the pan.

Ask your mom or dad to help you collect some mud and water. You'll find some at the bottom of a pond or ditch.

Pour the water and mud into your pond. Then lean a stick up the side. Animals that fall in can climb up it . . . so they don't drown!

Now sit back and wait. Your pond is already full of life. The mud at the bottom holds millions of tiny plants and animals. When they've grown bigger, you'll be able to see them.

After three weeks, dip a jar in the water.

Then look closely.You may see some amazing animals!

POND PANORAMA

Here are just a few of the animals you may find in your pond.

COMMON WATER STRIDER
An insect that skates on the surface looking for food such as drowned flies.

WATER FLEA
Lives just under the surface and feeds on small insects. It's about four hundredths of an inch (1 millimeter) long.

Toad tadpole

Frog tadpole

Newt tadpole

TADPOLES
Frog, newt, or toad spawn in your pond will turn into tadpoles. These turn into adult frogs, newts, and toads. Take them to a larger pond when they've grown.

STICKLEBACK
If you're lucky, some fish eggs may hatch out. Take the fish to a larger pond when they've grown.

MAYFLY LARVA
Many insects start life as eggs laid in mud. An egg turns into a young insect called a larva.
In early summer, the larva leaves the water and turns into a winged adult.

HYDRA
An animal that looks like a plant! It hangs from weeds waiting for food to drift into reach of its tentacles.

COMMON LEECH
A wormlike creature that clings to other animals and sucks their blood!

Most ponds are fed by streams or rainwater. You'll need to keep your smaller pond filled up with tap water, especially in summer. If you want larger pond animals to come and live in your wildlife refuge, ask your parents to build a garden pond.

TOADS

If you're lucky, a toad may move into your wildlife refuge.

Toads can be a lot of fun. You can even teach them to take food from your hand!

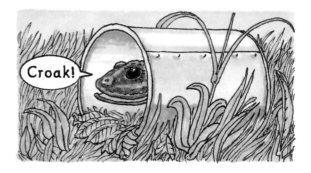

Make a home for your toad. Put some grass and leaves inside an old can. A toad will like this homemade home!

OLD TOAD FACT

Your toad may still be around when you've grown up. Toads live for up to 40 years!

FAT TOAD FACT

Toads can puff themselves up with air when they're frightened by predators. This makes animals such as snakes think they're too big to eat!

TOAD PIMPLE FACT

The lumps on a toad's skin contain a slime that tastes nasty. This sometimes saves toads from being eaten by birds!

TOAD EYEBALL FACT

Toads chew their food, such as worms, with their eyeball muscles. That's why they close their eyes when eating!

WHAT EATS WHAT?

Animals live by eating plants or each other.
Check what you've found out so far.

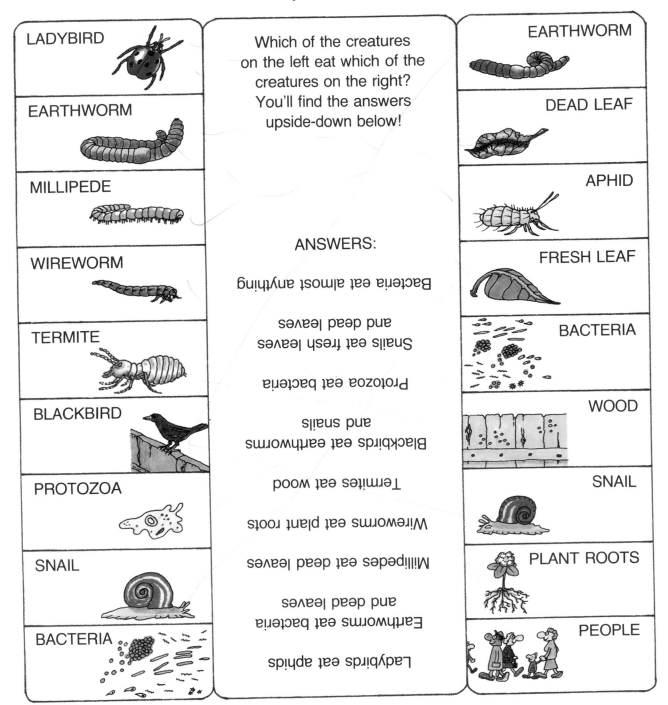

LADYBIRD

EARTHWORM

MILLIPEDE

WIREWORM

TERMITE

BLACKBIRD

PROTOZOA

SNAIL

BACTERIA

Which of the creatures
on the left eat which of the
creatures on the right?
You'll find the answers
upside-down below!

ANSWERS:

Bacteria eat almost anything

Snails eat fresh leaves
and dead leaves

Protozoa eat bacteria

Blackbirds eat earthworms
and snails

Termites eat wood

Wireworms eat plant roots

Millipedes eat dead leaves

Earthworms eat bacteria
and dead leaves

Ladybirds eat aphids

EARTHWORM

DEAD LEAF

APHID

FRESH LEAF

BACTERIA

WOOD

SNAIL

PLANT ROOTS

PEOPLE

MAKING NOTES

You can find out about small animals by studying them closely.

But . . . some animals are too small for you to see properly. A magnifying glass will help you to see them better.

You can buy a good one from a toy shop.

Get a notebook, too, and set out half of the pages like this . . .

DATE	TIME	ANIMALS	WHERE SEEN	COMMENTS
APRIL 2	10.30 am	Sowbugs	Under leaves	Lots of them
APRIL 2	11.00 am	Toad	Under a hedge	Looked sleepy
April 3	10.00 am	Centipede	Under a stone	20 pairs of legs
April 3	10.40 am	Boy next door	Treading on my plants	FATHEAD!

Use the other pages to draw the animals you see. You may be lucky and spot some creatures that nobody's ever seen before. New animals are being discovered all the time.

You might not be able to find out the names of the animals you've seen. Draw them anyway, and make up your own names for them!

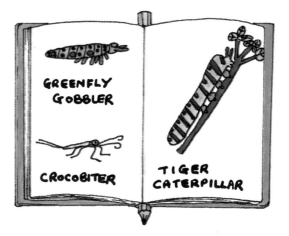

GREENFLY GOBBLER

CROCOBITER

TIGER CATERPILLAR

HANDLING SMALL ANIMALS

Just imagine what it would be like to be picked up by a great big hand from the sky!

If you need to pick up an animal to study it, do it gently.

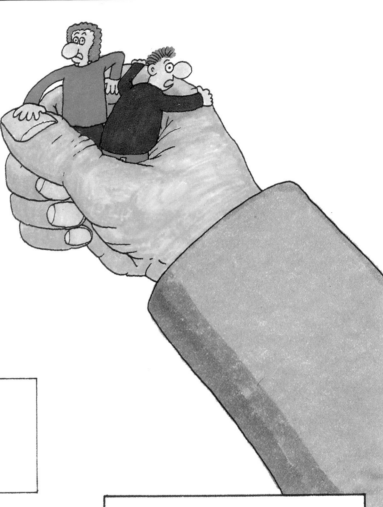

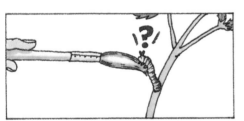

Pick up very small creatures with a leaf, spoon, or paintbrush.

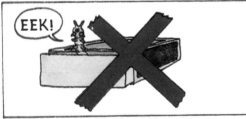

Don't put them in small matchboxes or jars.

Study them for only a short while. Then return them to where you found them.

BUTTERFLY WING FACT

Moths and butterflies have a fine powder on their wings that helps them to fly. Never pick up butterflies by their wings. You may damage them.

SHREWS, VOLES, AND MICE

Some animals produce milk for their young. These kinds of animals are called mammals. Human beings are mammals. So are shrews, voles, and mice.

Small mammals such as these make paths between the stems of plants. This keeps them partly hidden from flying predators such as hawks. You must keep very still and quiet if you want to see them. They might visit your wildlife refuge.

COMMON SHREW
This busy animal eats up to three times its own weight in insects every day!

PIGMY SHREW
An insect eater. It uses up its energy so quickly that it has to eat almost all the time!

FIELD VOLE
Eats insects and some plants. Voles store food underground to eat in winter.

WHITE-FOOTED MOUSE
Loves strawberries. Has poor eyesight. You can get very close to one if you creep up quietly.

FAT CATS

Shrews, voles, and mice can be food for larger animals such as owls and weasels.

Nowadays, small animals in gardens are more likely to be killed by cats. There are a lot more cats than owls or weasels.

Your cuddly pussycat could be more than it seems.

When you're not watching, it could be a dangerous killer!

Cats used to be wild creatures that hunted for food before they learned to live in people's houses. Most cats can't help hunting small animals. It's no use trying to stop them. Just one cat in your street will not kill too many animals. The problem is that such a lot of houses have cats. So . . . don't forget the damage to wildlife if you're thinking of getting a cat.

FAT CAT FACT

There are more cats than dogs living in the United States. Pet cats kill many millions of small animals and birds each year.

But cats don't need to kill for food because their owners feed them.

Cats will chase almost any small, moving thing!

AUTUMN

Late summer and autumn are the times when most trees and plants die down. Their leaves form a layer of leaf litter on the ground.

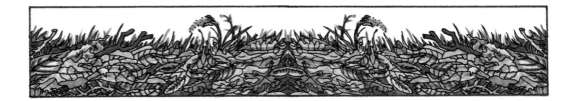

This leaf litter makes a new habitat for millions of animals and bacteria. Here are just three of them.

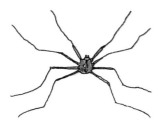

HARVESTMAN
A spider that hunts among leaves for insects. It doesn't spin a web.

BRISTLETAIL
Eats rotting plants.

EARTHWORM
Eats leaves and helps turn dead plants into new soil.

Before autumn is over, many dead plants have been eaten and turned into animal droppings.

The droppings and the remains of dead animals become mixed with dust to make new soil.

LEAF SKELETON FACT

Oak
leaf

Sometimes you can see leaves like this. Lots of insects such as caterpillars eat leaves. The veins of the leaves are hard to chew, so they aren't always eaten . . . leaving a leaf skeleton!

AUTUMN

Autumn is also the time when there are lots of seeds, berries, and nuts to eat.

Because there is so much food, this is the time when you'll find the most animals in your wildlife refuge.

Look out for wasps eating rotting fruit.

Are there any large trees nearby? If so, seeds and nuts may fall into your garden.

You may be lucky and see a squirrel on a nut hunt!

Walnut

SANTA CLAWS

But by late autumn, the plants are dying away and the food is running out.

Animals have to start preparing for winter.

WHAT ANIMALS DO IN WINTER

STAY IN EGG OR CHRYSALIS

Most adult insects die, but many young insects stay in eggs or in a chrysalis until spring.

Insect eggs under a stone

ZZZZ!

Butterfly chrysalis on a twig

CHEEP FLIGHTS!

MIGRATE

Birds that eat insects in summer have to fly away to a warmer country to find food in winter.

HIBERNATE

This is like a long, deep sleep. Animals don't need to eat when they hibernate. That means they don't have to go out to look for food so often. The dormouse sleeps about six months of the year!

ZZZZZ!

TWITTER!
CHUTTLE!
SQUAWK!
FLUTTER!
CHUCKLE!
CHIRP!

DIE OF COLD

Small animals die of cold very easily. Some birds huddle in groups to stay warm. Many mammals grow extra fur for warmth.

DIE OF HUNGER

It's hard for animals to find food when the ground is covered over with snow and frost. Worms, for instance, tunnel deep down below the frozen part of the soil.

EEK!

YOW!

WAP!

SUMMER

WINTER

WHAT YOU CAN DO IN WINTER

Only the strongest animals live through the winter. Birds will visit your wildlife refuge all year long. But when winter comes, they won't find so much to eat.

You can help some of them to survive by putting food out for them. Why not make a bird feeder?

HOW TO MAKE A BIRD FEEDER

FOOD FOR BIRDS

BREAD · BACON RIND

SEEDS · CAKE · SUET

COOKIES · CHEESE

And you can give birds a bowl of warm water on frosty days.

Nail an old wooden tray or a flat piece of wood to a tall post. Put food on it every day.

Birds will get used to seeing food in their feeder. If there's no food, some birds may wait too long for it and may die of cold. So don't forget to keep on feeding the birds.

Put the feeder high enough to be out of the reach of cats.

Some birds will eat only food on the ground. Remember to scatter some food there too.

Now sit back and wait for spring to begin all over again. Next year, your wildlife refuge will have more life in it than ever!

Every year, the small creatures, especially the worms, will help your wildlife refuge to grow.

More and more plants and animals will move in.

Then you can invite all your friends on wildlife safaris!

BUT DON'T GET LOST
IN THE JUNGLE!

FIND OUT MORE

Now that you've learned how to make a home for wildlife in your backyard, find out more about the wildlife in your area. Visit a park or nature center near your home and see how many different plants and animals you can spot.

Here are some books to look for in the library:

Endangered Animals, by Lynn M. Stone (Childrens Press, 1984)

Small Garden Animals, by Terry Jennings (Childrens Press, 1989)

What's Under That Rock?, by Stephen M. Hoffman (Macmillan, 1985)

Wildlife Alert, by Gene S. Stuart (National Geographic, 1980)

INDEX